The Rockwool Foundation Research Unit

Has Globalization Changed the Phillips Curve? Industry-Level Evidence on the Effect of the Unemployment Gap on Wages

Claus Aastrup Jensen

University Press of Southern Denmark
Odense 2009

Has Globalization Changed the Phillips Curve?
Industry-Level Evidence on the Effect of the Unemployment Gap on Wages

Study Paper No. 23

Published by:
© The Rockwool Foundation Research Unit and
University Press of Southern Denmark

Copying from this book is permitted only within
institutions that have agreements with CopyDan,
and only in accordance with the limitations laid
down in the agreement

Address:
The Rockwool Foundation Research Unit
Sejroegade 11
DK-2100 Copenhagen Oe

Telephone   +45 39 17 38 32

Fax   +45 39 20 52 19

E-mail   forskningsenheden@rff.dk

Home page   www.rff.dk

ISBN   978-87-90199-25-8
ISSN   0908-3979
March 2009
Print run: 300
Printed by   Special-Trykkeriet Viborg a-s

Price: 60.00 DKK, including 25% VAT

Foreword

In 2005 the Rockwool Foundation decided through their Research Unit to initiate a project that would investigate the significance of the immigration of foreign labour for the Danish labour market. A project of this type had become especially relevant following the expansion of the EU in 2004 to include a number of East European countries, and that relevance was further increased with the accession of Bulgaria and Romania to EU membership in 2007.

The Rockwool Foundation Research Unit then entered into an agreement to work on the project in cooperation with the Centre for Economic and Business Research (CEBR) at Copenhagen Business School. At CEBR, Research Director Nikolaj Malchow-Møller, Professor Jakob Roland Munch and Professor Jan Rose Skaksen carried out the enormous task of collecting and analysing the data that were accessible. These researchers are also the principal authors of a book on the project, *Det danske arbejdsmarked og EU-udvidelsen mod øst* (The Danish labour market and the eastward expansion of the EU), which is being published by Gyldendal simultaneously with the publication of this Study Paper.

In their work on the analyses and the production of the text of their book, the three authors received assistance from Claus Aastrup Jensen, a PhD student studying both at the Department of Business and Economics at the University of Southern Denmark and at CEBR. He undertook the important task of investigating the effect of immigration on wage formation in Denmark, examining in particular whether globalisation and immigration had made wage increases less sensitive to changes in the economic cycle, thus contributing to the flattening-out of the Philips curve experienced by Denmark and other industrialised countries in recent years. This Study Paper presents the work on the project that Claus Aastrup Jensen carried out.

At the Research Unit, Mai-britt Sejberg has undertaken the work of proofreading the manuscript and preparing the documents for printing, while Bent Jensen has been responsible for liaison with the University Press of Southern Denmark.

As always with the Research Unit's projects, this research has been carried out in complete academic independence and free from the influence of any party, including the Rockwool Foundation itself, who provided the necessary resources for the project.

The research group and I would like to extend our warmest thanks to the staff of the Foundation, including the Director, Elin Schmidt, and the Board, chaired by Tom Kähler, for their unfailing and generous support and cooperation.

Copenhagen, March 2009 *Torben Trancæs*

Contents

Abstract		7
1.	Introduction	9
2.	Previous Literature	13
3.	The Phillips Curve: A Theoretical Approach	17
3.1.	Decomposition technique	17
4.	Data	19
5.	Estimation Strategy	27
5.1.	Sensitivity of wages to the unemployment gap	27
5.2.	Globalization and the slope of the Phillips curve	28
6.	Empirical Results	29
6.1.	Estimation and decomposition of the slope of the Phillips curve	29
6.2.	Does globalization affect the slope of the Phillips curve?	31
7.	Conclusion	35
References		37
Publications in English from the Rockwool Foundation Research Unit		39
The Rockwool Foundation Research Unit on the Internet		42

Has Globalization Changed the Phillips Curve? Industry-Level Evidence on the Effect of the Unemployment Gap on Wages

Claus Aastrup Jensen[♣]

Abstract

It has recently been argued that the flattening of the Phillips curve, observed in many industrial countries over the last two decades, is due to globalization. However, so far only a very limited number of studies in the existing literature have managed to analyze the effect of globalization on the Phillips curve directly, and none of these are using industry-level data. In the present paper, I estimate industry-specific Phillips curves for Denmark to test whether the finding of a weaker link between wages and the unemployment gap is due to changes within industries or should instead be ascribed to changes in the relative sizes of industries. In addition to this, I test how far globalization through a variety of channels influences the slope of the Phillips curve. Based on input-output tables and linked employer-employee data, I find that the decline of the sensitivity of wages to the unemployment gap is caused almost entirely by changes in the slopes of industry-specific Phillips curves. Furthermore, I find that industries with an easier access to international outsourcing show weaker wage responses to the unemployment gap, whereas access to import of foreign final goods and foreign labour seem to have no effect on the slope of the Phillips curve.

Keywords: Phillips curve, trade, labour immigration, industry-level data

JEL Classification: F16, J64

[♣] Contact: Claus Aastrup Jensen, caj@sam.sdu.dk, www.cebr.dk/caj, address: University of Southern Denmark, Department of Business and Economics, Campusvej 55, 5230 Odense M, Denmark.

1. Introduction

Since the beginning of the 1990s, many developed countries have experienced simultaneous low and falling inflation and low unemployment at odds with the properties of a standard Phillips curve. While most empirical analyses in the context of traditional Phillips curves explain the lower sensitivity of inflation to unemployment by changes in monetary policy, a still increasing number of studies instead link the lower slope of the Phillips curve to globalization. In this light, several recent speeches by policymakers have addressed the issue of whether globalization has changed the role of domestic factors in shaping the inflation process and, if so, what are the economic consequences of reduced sensitivity of inflation to fluctuations in the unemployment rate. On the plus side, it is argued that a flatter Phillips curve implies that an overheated economy will tend to generate a smaller increase in inflation potentially prolonging cycles of economic upswing. On the negative side, however, a flatter Phillips curve also carries the implication that, for a given degree of inflation persistence, reducing inflation involves a higher sacrifice ratio than otherwise, namely it requires enduring a longer period of unemployment above the natural rate for every desired percentage point of reduction in inflation (Bean, 2006; Mishkin, 2007).

In this paper, I estimate industry-specific Phillips curves to analyze the causes of the flattening of the aggregate Phillips curve observed in Denmark, and in many other industrial countries, over the last two decades. In contrast to most of the previous studies, which typically use a modified Phillips curve specification to investigate the inflation-unemployment trade-off between countries over time, the estimation approach presented in this paper instead follows the conventional Phillips curve theory asserting that the rate of wage changes is explained in terms of the unemployment rate (Phillips, 1958).

The estimation method presented in the paper is novel by estimating industry-specific Phillips curves. This in turn allows me to analyze the causes of the declining sensitivity of wages to the unemployment gap by decomposing the change in the slope of the Phillips curve into parts that can be ascribed to changes within industries and changes in employment shares between industries, respectively. Furthermore, the method allows me to analyze how far different channels of economic openness influence the slope of the Phillips curve across industries. To the best of my knowledge, so far none of these analyses have been done for any country in the existing literature.

In the first of two stages of the empirical analysis, changes in industry-specific wages are related to the unemployment gap of the economy to generate measures of wage responses to fluctuations of unemployment for every industry. Using a standard decomposition technique, this Phillips curve specification allows me to decompose changes in the slope of the aggregate Phillips curve into parts that can be ascribed to changes in slopes of industry-specific Phillips curves and changes in employment shares between industries, respectively. Empirical evidence of such "within-industry effect" and "between-industry effect", related to the slope of the aggregate Phillips curve, is provided using input-output tables from national accounts and linked employer-employee data for Denmark.

In the second stage of the empirical analysis, the effect of globalization on the slope of the aggregate Phillips curve is analyzed by relating the slopes of the industry-specific Phillips curves to a variety of channels through which globalization may be expected to weaken the relationship between wages and unemployment. Specifically, I distinguish between three channels of economic openness in the analyses: import of foreign final goods and services (import); import of foreign intermediate goods (outsourcing); and utilization of foreign labour (labour immigration).

First, it could be argued that import of foreign final goods may weaken the relationship between wage changes and the unemployment gap essentially because trade with other countries acts as a "buffer" to balance domestic demand and supply, helping curb to wage fluctuations. Second, international outsourcing is another channel through which globalization is likely to affect wage responses to the unemployment gap. Given the availability of production factors that are produced abroad and are easily importable, it is possible for firms to replace domestic intermediates with imported intermediates potentially restraining wage changes to fluctuations in the unemployment gap. Finally, yet another channel of globalization which could affect responses of wages to the unemployment gap is labour immigration. Although labour markets are highly protected compared with the openness of goods and service markets, employment of foreign labour may still be an important source for reducing wage pressures in periods with labour shortage.

To preview the results: I find that the sensitivity of wages to the unemployment gap has declined considerably in most industries in Denmark since the beginning of the 1990s. Especially for industries in the construction and manufacturing sectors, the tendency towards low wage increases at high rates of unemployment has been striking. It is shown that the decline in the sensitivity of wages to the unemployment gap is caused almost entirely by changes in the slopes of industry-specific Phillips curves, while changes in employment shares between industries are of limited importance. Furthermore, with respect to the influence of globalization on the slope of the Phillips curve, I find that manufacturing industries with an easier access to international outsourcing show weaker responses of wages to the unemployment gap, whereas the access to import of foreign final goods and foreign labour has no effect on the slope of the Phillips curve. However, it is important to mention that these results are not particularly robust and that, hence, there are a number of caveats to my conclusions.

The paper is organized as follows. Section 2 reviews previous studies analyzing channels through which globalization might be able to affect the Phillips curve.

In Section 3, I present the decomposition of the slope of the Phillips curve in the context of an industry-specific Phillips curve specification, and discuss theoretically how globalization may affect responses of wages to the unemployment gap. Data applied in the analyses are described in Section 4. In Section 5, I outline the estimation procedure and the assumptions needed for providing empirical evidence on the decomposition, and for testing the effect of globalization on the slope of the Phillips curve for the Danish economy. Section 6 contains the estimation results. Finally, Section 7 concludes.

2. Previous Literature

A substantial number of studies have analyzed the flattening of the Phillips curve observed in many industrial countries over the last two decades. There are serious disagreements in the literature on whether the increasing trade interdependencies in global markets and growing exchanges of production factors among countries have weakened the linkage between inflation and unemployment. While some studies find that global factors have supplanted the role of domestic measures of excess demand as the key determinant of the slope of the Phillips curve, others argue that the observed flattening of the Phillips curve is due to institutional and (monetary) policy changes, but not globalization.

In discussing how globalization affects the Phillips curve, it has been common to focus on a number of channels of economic openness. Particularly, three broad channels of economic openness have been analyzed in the theoretical literature each representing partial effects that may weaken the relationship between wage changes and the rate of unemployment captured by the standard Phillips curve.

The first channel of economic openness which is emphasized in the theoretical literature as a carrier of globalization effects on wage changes is importation of foreign final goods and services. Increased import from other countries acts as a buffer to balance the domestic demand and supply of goods and services, and helps restrain workers' wage demands related to excess demand in goods and service markets. Therefore, a higher import induces wages to become less sensitive to changes in the domestic rate of unemployment. Theoretically, Razin and Yuen (2002) show that trade at the goods market flattens the Phillips curve.

The second channel of economic openness through which globalization may affect the Phillips curve is international outsourcing. Globalization enhances the opportunities for firms to substitute imports for domestic production inputs by shifting their production to plants in other countries. As such opportunities for substitution increase, firms become less willing to grant wage increases that would impair their cost competitiveness, even in the face of tight domestic labour markets. Therefore, opportunities for substitution increase the degree of competition between workers in the home country and workers abroad, reducing the pressures on wages at low rates of unemployment (Rodrik, 1997).

In addition to the import and outsourcing effects, the third channel of economic openness often stressed in the theoretical literature, through which globalization may affect the link between wage changes and unemployment, relates to labour mobility. In general, access to foreign labour offsets pressures on wages through increases in the labour supply potentially leading to lower wages for given rates of unemployment. This implies that increases in the rate of utilization of foreign labour flatten the Phillips curve. These effects are analyzed theoretically by Bentolila *et al.* (2007) and Razin and Binyamini (2007).

A large number of studies have tested the influence of the distinct channels of economic openness on the slope of the Phillips curve empirically. With respect to the two channels on international trade ('import' and 'outsourcing'), there exists evidence that trade affects the Phillips curve. In an often-cited study, Borio and Filardo (2007) show that there is a link between the smaller Phillips curves' slopes observed for many countries and the spread of globalization. Specifically, by estimating country-specific Phillips curves for 16 OECD countries over the periods 1980-1992 and 1993-2005, they relate national inflation rates and output gaps to a trade-weighted global output gap and find that in the more recent period there has been a decline in the slope of the Phillips curve in most countries due to the growing role of global factors. Another study that analyzes the effect of trade on the Phillips curve is Helbling *et al.* (2006) using data on 8 OECD countries over the period 1960-2004. In the context of a modified Phillips curve specification, relating national inflation rates to the output gap and to trade openness, this study provides evidence indicating that increases in international trade have contributed to the declining slope of many countries' Phillips curves over the past two decades (see also Dexter *et al.*, 2005; Pain *et al.*, 2006).

However, many studies still find the cross-country evidence regarding the effects of international trade on the slope of the Phillips curve being mixed (see, e.g., Temple, 2002; Bowdler, 2003; Ball, 2006; Ihrig *et al.*, 2007). The main impression from all these studies is that trade has, at most, a small effect on the sensitivity of wages, alternatively inflation, to unemployment. One of the most influential studies that empirically rejects the claim that trade weakens the slope of the Phillips curve is Temple (2002). This study relates trade openness to the different measures of inflation-output trade-off for a large group of developed countries over the period 1948-1988 and finds that the empirical support for a correlation between openness and the slope of the Phillips curve is not well-established. Bowdler (2003) has later extended this study by allowing the strength of the relationship between international trade and the inflation-output ratio to depend on the exchange rate regime. Using data for the period 1948-1998, the study finds limited evidence that the decline in the inflation-output trade-off is due to trade openness. In fact, the evidence for the post-1980 period suggests that amongst countries maintaining flexible exchange rate regimes, the effect of openness has been to increase the slope of the Phillips curve.[1] Two other studies that are often mentioned in the literature as being important empirical contributions are Ball (2006) and Ihrig *et al.* (2007). From data on OECD countries for periods from the mid-1970s to 2005, these studies also find limited support for the hypothesis that the flattening of the Phillips curve is an effect of recent decades' increase in trade openness.

---

[1] These findings are supported by Rogoff (2006) who argues that increases in international competition due to higher trade flows between countries should in principle steepen, rather than flatten, the Phillips curve: firms need to revise their prices more frequently, as the cost of keeping prices fixed at the wrong level increases.

Regarding the third channel of economic openness, the empirical evidence is more limited. One of the few studies that analyzes the effect of labour flows on the slope of the Phillips curve is Bentolila *et al.* (2007), who set up a New Keynesian Phillips curve accounting for labour immigration effects. Specifically, the study extends a standard expectation-augmented Phillips curve (that relates inflation to the future and lagged inflation, the unemployment rate and imported input prices) by adding a further explanatory variable to the specification: the gap between the unemployment rates of native and immigrant workers. By using data for Spain for the period 1982-1996, the study estimates the effect of this "relative immigrant unemployment" on the inflation-unemployment trade-off, and finds that the Spanish Phillips curve has become much flatter over the last two decades due to large immigration flows that occurred in Spain during the 1990s.

While there is substantial empirical work on the effects of globalization on countries' Phillips curve slopes, the effects at the industrial level have received much less attention in the empirical literature. To my knowledge, so far the only other study that analyzes the impact of globalization on the Phillips curve at a more disaggregate level is Bentolila *et al.* (2007). This study estimates Phillips curves for three industries in Spain: manufacturing, construction, and services, finding that the effect of utilization of foreign labour on the slope of the national Phillips curve is larger for those industries with higher intensity of immigrant labour. Two related studies dealing – though not directly – with the link between globalization and the Phillips curve are Gamber & Hung (2001) and Helbling *et al.* (2006). These studies investigate the role played by trade openness on producer prices using industrial-level data for the US and a group of OECD countries. Both studies find changes in producer prices to be negatively related to industry-level import penetration, implying that the effect of enhanced trade openness has increased considerably in many industrial countries over the past two decades.

The general conclusion from the literature seems to be that there is a large number of cross-country studies testing the influence of the various channels of economic openness on the slope of the Phillips curve. However, so far only a very limited number of studies have managed to test the impact of globalization on the slope of the Phillips curve at a more disaggregate level, while no previous study has been able to distinguish between different types of economic openness. In this light, the present paper contributes to the existing literature by estimating industry-specific Phillips curves determining the influence of different effects of globalization on the slope of the aggregate Phillips curve of Denmark.

3. The Phillips Curve: A Theoretical Approach

In this section, I specify an industry-level Phillips curve that allows me to rewrite the standard Phillips curve as an average of industry-specific Phillips curves of the entire economy. From the industry-level Phillips curve setup, I test to what extent changes in the sensitivity of wages to the unemployment gap are driven by changes within industries and changes in employment shares between industries, respectively, using a standard decomposition technique. Furthermore, I use the setup to test the importance of three channels of economic openness through which globalization may be able to affect the slope of the Phillips curve. The data applied in the empirical analyses are described in Section 4, while Section 5 presents the empirical strategy.

3.1. Decomposition technique

The specification of the industry-level Phillips curve is built on the conventional Phillips curve, asserting that the rate of wage increases is explained in terms of the unemployment rate (Phillips, 1958). I modify the original formulation by including the rate of real wage growth and the unemployment gap as explanatory variables:

$$\Delta w_t = \alpha_t - \beta\left(u_t - u_t^*\right) \tag{1}$$

where Δw_t is the change of the real wage rate in year t; α_t is the rate of the real wage growth in year t; and $(u_t - u_t^*)$ is the unemployment gap in year t given by the deviation of the actual unemployment rate from its structural rate in that particular year.

Since the objective of this paper is to analyze the linkage between wage changes and the unemployment gap at the industrial level, I focus on industry-specific Phillips curves. To do this, I assume that there are n industries in the economy and that there for each industry exists a Phillips curve. In the present analysis, the Phillips curve for industry i is given as in (2), where the change in the real wage for the industry is determined by the growth rate of the real wage for the industry, α_{it}, and the unemployment gap for the entire economy:

$$\Delta w_{it} = \alpha_{it} - \beta_i\left(u_t - u_t^*\right) \tag{2}$$

By using (2), I assume that the relationship between the real wage and the unemployment gap for the economy is given by a weighted average of the n industry-specific Phillips curves. This allows me to rewrite (1) into an expression that links up the aggregate Phillips curve and the specific Phillips curves for all industries (see also Bentolila et al., 2007). In the present analysis, I assume that Δw_t is the rate of change of the real wage for the entire economy in year t, while θ_{it} is the share of industry i in total employment of the economy in year t and β_i is the slope of the Phillips curve for industry i:

$$\Delta w_t = \sum_{i=1}^{n} \theta_{it} \alpha_{it} - \sum_{i=1}^{n} \theta_{it} \beta_i \left(u_t - u_t^* \right) \quad (3)$$

This equation shows that the change in the real wage for the economy as a whole depends on two terms; the growth rates of real wages for the n industries and the national unemployment gap. Of particular interest to my study, it follows that the slope of the aggregate Phillips curve is a weighted average of the slopes of the Phillips curve for all industries in the economy. This implies that a change in the slope of the aggregate Phillips curve are due to changes in the slopes of industry-specific Phillips curves and changes in the employment shares between industries, respectively. I analyze the importance of these two parts by adapting a standard decomposition technique to obtain a breakdown of the change of the slope of the aggregate Phillips curve. Formally, the change in β between two periods can be decomposed as in (4), where the change in the slope of the Phillips curve is determined by changes in β_i and θ_i:

$$\Delta \beta = \sum_{i=1}^{n} \overline{\theta}_i \Delta \beta_i + \sum_{i=1}^{n} \Delta \theta_i \left(\overline{\beta}_i - \overline{\beta} \right) \quad (4)$$

The first term on the right-hand side in (4) represents the "within-industry effect". It is the contribution to the change in the slope of the aggregate Phillips curve due to changes in the slopes of industry-specific Phillips curves. This term is calculated as the changes in the slopes of the Phillips curves for the n industries between two periods of time (1 and 2), $\Delta \beta_i = \beta_{i,2} - \beta_{i,1}$, weighted by their average shares of employment in the entire economy, $\overline{\theta}_i$. The second term in (4) is the "between-industry effect", which gives the change in the slope of the aggregate Phillips curve that stems from changes in employment shares between industries. It is calculated as the changes in the shares of employment for the n industries between two periods of time, $\Delta \theta_i = \theta_{i,2} - \theta_{i,1}$, multiplied by the difference between the average slope of the industry-specific Phillips curve for each industry and the average slope of the Phillips curve for the economy as a whole, $(\overline{\beta}_i - \overline{\beta}_i)$.

From (4), I am able to derive the "within-industry effects" and "between-industry effects" from the decomposition using the employment shares and the estimated values of β_i for each industry. Furthermore, I can use the estimated values of β_i to test the influence of globalization on the slope of the Phillips curve by relating the changes in β_i to measures of the three channels of economic openness.

4. Data

From the Integrated Database of Labour Market Research (IDA), I hold information on all Danish residents for the period 1980-2006.[2] From the IDA, I first use information about individual hourly wage rates for workers to calculate the annual wage changes for every industry in the private sector for the period 1980-2006. The analyses are restricted to include only full-time workers in the age group of 18-65 years, and industries in the private sector (96 industries) are classified according to the standard 130-classification in the Danish national accounts. Second, data on the unemployment gap – measured as the difference between the actual and structural rate of unemployment – are taken from the Danish Economic Council. The Danish Economic Council estimates the rate of structural unemployment on the basis of the observed variation in wage inflation and unemployment, using a comprehensive macroeconometric model building on an expectations-augmented Phillips curve specification and the Kalman filter.[3] Third, the measures of international trade ("import" and "outsourcing") are constructed for every industry in the private sector using input-output tables from the Danish national accounts, whereas the measure of utilization of foreign labour ("labour immigration") builds on IDA data.

In the first stage of the empirical analysis, I use data on the average wage changes for industries and the unemployment gap for the entire economy to estimate the sensitivity of wages to the unemployment gap for every industry. The average wage increase for industry i in year t is calculated as the average wage increase for the wage earners who were employed in industry i in both year t-1 and t. Adjustment for inflation is accomplished by dividing the average wage increase for industry i by the change in the Consumer Price Index of the economy for the same year. As mentioned earlier, the unemployment gap is defined as the difference between the actual and structural rate of unemployment of the economy. According to the standard Phillips curve, I expect wage changes to be negatively affected by the unemployment gap, though the strength of this relationship to some extent may vary across industries. In Table 1, I present descriptive statistics for the average number of full-time workers and for the average real wage changes for the periods 1980-1992 and 1993-2006 for each of the 96 industries included in the empirical analyses:[4]

---

[2] For more details on the IDA, see Abowd and Kramarz (1999).
[3] For more details on the approach of the Danish Economic Council with regard to estimating the structural rate of unemployment of Denmark, see Danish Economic Council (2008).
[4] Due to a change in the calculation of wages in 1993, which affects the computation of wage increases between 1992 and 1993, I distinguish between two sub-periods of almost equal sizes in the empirical analyses, namely the periods of 1980-1992 and 1993-2006.

Table 1: Summary statistics of industry size and change of wages

Industries:	(1) Number of employees (Average) 1980-1992	(2) Number of employees (Average) 1993-2006	(3) Change of wage (Average) 1980-1992	(4) Change of wage (Average) 1993-2006
Agriculture	16,780	15,255	2.19%	3.76%
Horticulture, orchards	5,297	6,077	3.19%	2.59%
Agricultural services, landscape gardeners	4,696	6,193	1.08%	1.99%
Forestry	3,084	2,194	2.22%	0.72%
Fishing	3,451	2,429	1.69%	2.18%
Extraction of crude petroleum, natural gas	826	1,617	4.61%	3.76%
Extraction of gravel, clay, stone and salt	2,169	1,703	1.59%	1.87%
Production of meat and meat products	23,104	21,334	3.15%	1.82%
Processing of fish and fish products	7,712	6,258	2.54%	1.43%
Processing of fruit and vegetables	2,482	2,194	2.19%	2.49%
Manufacture of vegetable and animal oils	2,152	826	2.76%	2.88%
Manufacture of dairy products	9,987	9,742	2.58%	2.22%
Manufacture of starch and sugar products	8,226	9,877	2.38%	2.30%
Manufacture of bread, cakes and biscuits	3,691	4,277	2.10%	2.12%
Bakers' shops	5,161	5,210	5.99%	4.47%
Manufacture of sugar	2,372	1,148	2.44%	2.57%
Manufacture of beverages	8,515	5,305	1.93%	2.03%
Manufacture of tobacco products	1,968	1,221	2.10%	2.55%
Manufacture of textiles and textile products	11,970	7,483	2.45%	1.95%
Manufacture of wearing apparel	10,080	4,063	2.46%	2.64%
Manufacture of leather and leather products	2,413	1,078	2.27%	2.08%
Manufacture of wood and wood products	10,554	13,476	2.45%	2.32%
Manufacture of pulp, paper and paper products	8,722	8,139	2.47%	1.66%
Publishing of newspapers	8,928	6,952	1.97%	1.99%
Publishing activities, excluding newspapers	4,787	7,684	2.59%	3.05%
Printing activities	16,553	12,607	3.76%	2.50%
Manufacture of refined petroleum products	882	771	2.68%	3.56%
Manufacture of industrial gases	774	682	-0.28%	2.24%
Manufacture of fertilizers	1,104	431	2.30%	2.25%
Manufacture of plastics and synthetic rubber	752	509	2.18%	2.14%
Manufacture of agro-chemical products	110	692	3.99%	1.22%
Manufacture of paints, printing ink and mastics	2,923	2,203	2.82%	2.72%
Manufacture of pharmaceuticals	10,970	13,172	2.95%	3.14%
Manufacture of detergents	3,683	5,090	2.63%	2.50%
Manufacture of rubber products	9,505	9,104	2.33%	2.15%
Manufacture of other plastic products	6,003	8,106	2.47%	2.57%
Manufacture of glass and ceramic goods	5,222	4,368	2.25%	2.09%
Manufacture of cement, bricks, tiles, flags	2,405	1,507	1.80%	2.21%
Manufacture of concrete and cement products	12,096	11,117	2.02%	2.17%
Manufacture of basic ferrous metals	2,108	1,217	0.84%	3.44%
First processing of iron and steel	1,054	2,842	2.49%	2.36%
Manufacture of basic non-ferrous metals	639	1,797	3.01%	2.05%
Casting of metal products	1,115	1,202	3.02%	1.83%
Manufacture of construct. materials of metal	23,729	23,004	3.38%	2.94%
Manufacture of hand tools, metal packaging	14,898	15,810	2.82%	2.54%
Manufacture of marine engines, compressors	30,425	20,607	2.74%	3.06%
Manufacture of other general machinery	5,457	17,878	3.38%	2.85%
Manufacture of agricultural machinery	5,876	5,025	2.98%	2.70%
Manufacture of machinery for industries	14,688	14,596	3.69%	3.26%
Manufacture of domestic appliances	4,149	4,437	2.57%	2.04%
Manufacture of office machinery	2,226	1,609	3.63%	2.86%
Manufacture of other electrical machinery	15,014	17,346	3.15%	2.66%

To be continued ......

Table 1 continued: Summary statistics of industry size and change of wages

	(1)	(2)	(3)	(4)
	Number of employees (Average)		Change of wage (Average)	
Industries:	1980-1992	1993-2006	1980-1992	1993-2006
Manufacture of communication equipment	11,134	9,738	2.64%	2.76%
Manufacture of medical and optical instruments	11,895	14,144	3.17%	2.84%
Manufacture of motor vehicles	5,049	6,413	3.26%	3.19%
Building and repairing of ships and boats	14,655	7,589	3.96%	3.32%
Manufacture of transport equipment excl. ships	2,012	2,424	3.24%	3.16%
Manufacture of furniture	18,178	20,074	3.13%	2.41%
Manufacture of toys, gold and silver articles	6,016	6,432	2.52%	2.74%
Construction and maintenance of buildings	121,004	130,456	3.70%	4.47%
Sale of motor vehicles, motorcycles	25,771	27,417	4.52%	4.84%
Repair and maintenance of motor vehicles	8,875	10,241	5.05%	3.87%
Service stations	2,803	3,476	1.47%	2.06%
Wholesale and commercial trade, ex. vehicles	117,918	127,601	2.74%	3.39%
Retail trade of food	25,936	27,983	3.78%	4.17%
Department stores	11,577	14,066	3.68%	5.19%
Retail sale of pharmaceutical goods	4,654	6,386	4.33%	4.20%
Retail sale of clothing, footwear	11,061	13,786	4.15%	4.79%
Other retail sale, repair work	25,299	38,764	3.93%	4.09%
Hotels	9,391	11,346	2.62%	2.61%
Restaurants	17,370	23,068	0.99%	1.34%
Transport via railways	18,044	9,550	1.97%	2.43%
Other scheduled passenger land transport	10,252	11,999	1.09%	1.59%
Taxi operation and coach services	4,826	7,755	-0.90%	-0.98%
Freight transport by road and via pipelines	20,011	24,743	1.09%	1.19%
Air transport	9,791	9,293	3.70%	3.19%
Cargo handling, harbors, travel agencies	9,824	14,917	2.15%	2.91%
Activities of other transport agencies	7,513	10,851	4.61%	4.49%
Post and telecommunication	20,489	41,524	1.64%	2.89%
Monetary intermediation	44,743	41,158	4.22%	3.72%
Other financial intermediation	6,094	8,224	3.61%	3.49%
Life insurance and pension funding	1,204	2,390	4.41%	3.64%
Non-life insurance	13,359	11,601	3.98%	3.50%
Activities auxiliary to financial intermediates	1,363	3,427	4.83%	3.09%
Real estate agents	2,504	7,088	4.32%	4.73%
Dwellings	11,270	11,633	1.84%	1.77%
Letting of non-residential buildings	103	1,911	1.76%	1.28%
Renting of machinery and equipment	1,706	4,062	1.96%	2.65%
Software consultancy and supply	9,440	20,684	3.90%	4.03%
Research and development	5,829	9,433	2.40%	2.75%
Firms of lawyers	5,533	7,367	5.33%	3.67%
Accounting, book-keeping, auditing	12,369	13,872	6.66%	5.35%
Consulting engineers, architects	19,746	30,499	3.19%	2.51%
Advertising	4,726	7,322	4.14%	4.43%
Industrial cleaning	6,825	10,600	2.28%	1.52%
Other business activities	15,344	26,583	2.61%	3.00%
Total:	1,076,993	1,199,354	3.07%	3.18%

Notes: The number of employees in columns (1) and (2) is computed as a simple average of the number of full-time workers for each industry for the periods 1980-1992 and 1993-2006. The change of wages in columns (3) and (4) is computed as a simple average of nominal wages, deflated by the Consumer Price Index, for full-time workers for each industry for the two periods.

For the Danish economy, Figure 1 overleaf displays the evolution of the change of the national average real wage and the unemployment gap, respectively. During the 1980s, there was a distinct inverse relationship between the rate of the real wage change and the unemployment gap consistent with the standard Phillips curve. However, since the beginning of the 1990s, the real wage increases have become less sensitive to the changes in the unemployment gap.

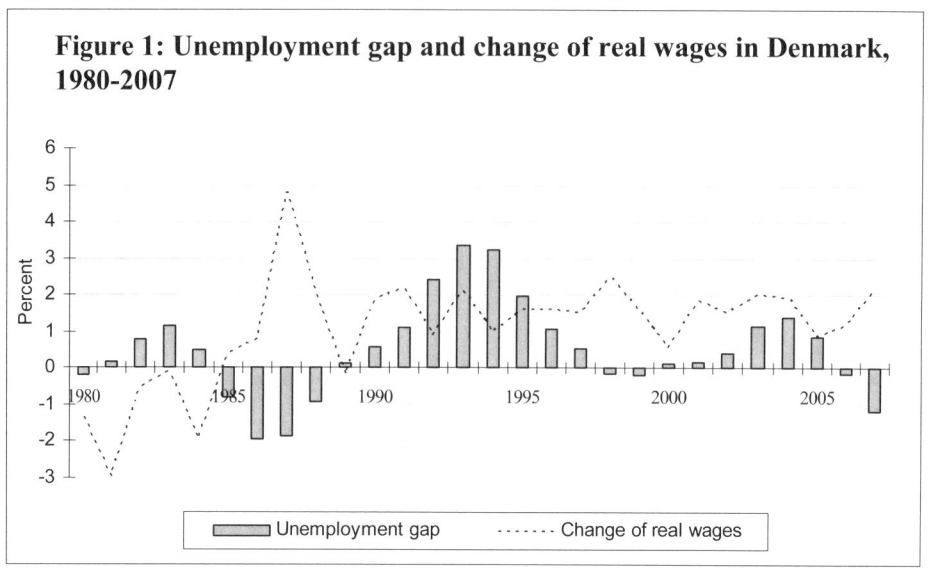

Figure 1: Unemployment gap and change of real wages in Denmark, 1980-2007

Notes: The unemployment gap is defined as the difference between the actual and structural rate of unemployment in Denmark.

Specifically, the unemployment gap has decreased by 1-2%, while the annual increases of the real wage in the same period have remained close to 2%. Thus, there is a tendency for the slope of the Phillips curve to decline over the period in the analyses.

In addition to the two variables depicted in Figure 1, I include three measures of economic openness in the analyses to test the influence of globalization on the linkage between the change of industry-specific wages and the unemployment gap of the economy (estimated in the second stage of the empirical analysis). Two of the measures deal with international trade in terms of the shares of import and outsourcing in production for every industry, which I compute from the input-output tables in the Danish national accounts. With respect to the share of import, this is calculated as the value of import of foreign final goods and services divided by the value of production for each industry. Similarly, the share of outsourcing is calculated as the value of imported foreign inputs for production divided by the value of production for each industry. Due to data restrictions on the measure of outsourcing for some industries, I restrict the analyses on globalization to include only industries in the manufacturing sector (see Munch and Skaksen, 2008). Finally, the third measure of globalization, labour immigration, is calculated as the number of immigrants – individuals who are born outside Denmark with non-Danish parents – in full-time employment divided by the total number of full-time workers for each industry.

In Table 2 on page 24-25, I present descriptive statistics for the average shares of import and outsourcing to production, and for the average share of foreign labour in total employment, for the periods 1980-1992 and 1993-2004 for each of the 54 manufacturing industries in Denmark.[5] It appears that the share of import of foreign final goods and services in production has increased in most industries between the two periods, while the increase in the import of production inputs from other countries has been more limited and divergent across industries. Moreover, it shows that Denmark has experienced an increase in the utilization of foreign labour between the two periods, although the development of the employment share of immigrants has been different between the industries.

In general, the data show that the Danish economy has become more open over the last two decades, while the slope of the aggregate Phillips curve in the same period has declined considerably. However, it is less certain whether the simultaneous appearance of the moderate wage increases and low unemployment also takes place in the same way across industries, and to what extent the change of this relationship should be related to globalization. The estimation procedure used for testing these important issues is described in the next section.

---

[5] Because data on the Danish input-output tables are only available up to 2004, some of the following analyses on globalization effects are conducted on the basis of data for the period 1980-2004.

Table 2: Summary statistics of measures of economic openness in manufacturing industries

Manufacturing industries:	(1) Share of import (Average)		(3) Share of outsourcing (Average)	(4)	(5) Share of labour immigration (Average)	(6)
	1980-1992	1993-2004	1980-1992	1993-2004	1980-1992	1993-2004
Extraction of crude petroleum, natural gas	7.81%	0.04%	1.73%	1.13%	4.14%	5.23%
Extraction of gravel, clay, stone and salt	3.17%	2.55%	6.35%	9.92%	0.98%	0.87%
Production of meat and meat products	1.03%	4.54%	3.05%	5.79%	2.72%	7.00%
Processing of fish and fish products	5.32%	3.85%	9.30%	18.79%	2.88%	9.39%
Processing of fruit and vegetables	28.19%	43.94%	16.81%	21.23%	2.33%	4.05%
Manufacture of vegetable and animal oils	2.76%	4.90%	11.51%	30.95%	2.67%	2.90%
Manufacture of dairy products	1.47%	4.12%	3.64%	6.08%	1.45%	2.29%
Manufacture of starch and sugar products	13.94%	15.50%	17.56%	23.16%	4.21%	5.28%
Manufacture of bread, cakes and biscuits	8.16%	10.01%	12.47%	17.13%	8.92%	8.71%
Bakers' shops	0.00%	0.00%	6.23%	10.58%	1.72%	3.11%
Manufacture of sugar	0.31%	0.42%	5.53%	5.10%	2.07%	2.01%
Manufacture of beverages	16.40%	17.21%	10.15%	15.66%	2.75%	3.12%
Manufacture of tobacco products	9.37%	3.92%	13.85%	12.19%	2.74%	3.35%
Manufacture of textiles and textile products	24.43%	35.18%	32.65%	30.24%	3.70%	6.36%
Manufacture of wearing apparel	64.68%	135.66%	25.09%	31.60%	3.44%	4.86%
Manufacture of leather and leather products	66.37%	140.49%	32.83%	37.30%	3.55%	7.30%
Manufacture of wood and wood products	2.16%	3.89%	24.06%	23.78%	2.71%	4.65%
Manufacture of pulp, paper and paper products	6.02%	7.57%	31.01%	29.09%	3.33%	3.31%
Publishing of newspapers	0.04%	0.25%	11.46%	10.28%	1.51%	1.69%
Publishing activities, excluding newspapers	0.19%	6.81%	11.65%	5.86%	2.99%	2.48%
Printing activities	2.28%	2.49%	18.61%	17.48%	1.83%	2.34%
Manufacture of refined petroleum products	23.79%	13.14%	1.36%	3.17%	3.21%	3.15%
Manufacture of industrial gases	0.38%	0.91%	21.09%	9.69%	2.92%	3.90%
Manufacture of fertilizers	8.20%	2.15%	35.28%	39.39%	2.50%	2.76%
Manufacture of plastics and synthetic rubber	0.71%	1.08%	40.12%	34.17%	8.29%	7.31%
Manufacture of agro-chemical products	1.21%	2.80%	22.75%	31.55%	2.83%	2.02%
Manufacture of paints, printing ink and mastics	0.88%	2.88%	33.05%	38.33%	7.06%	6.75%
Manufacture of pharmaceuticals	7.81%	6.66%	23.15%	18.07%	4.13%	4.77%

To be continued ....

Table 2 continued: Summary statistics of measures of economic openness in manufacturing industries

Manufacturing industries:	(1) Share of import (Average) 1980-1992	(2) Share of import (Average) 1993-2004	(3) Share of outsourcing (Average) 1980-1992	(4) Share of outsourcing (Average) 1993-2004	(5) Share of labour immigration (Average) 1980-1992	(6) Share of labour immigration (Average) 1993-2004
Manufacture of detergents	17.03%	19.29%	34.34%	35.13%	7.67%	4.63%
Manufacture of rubber products	1.90%	2.14%	33.26%	33.08%	6.31%	6.01%
Manufacture of other plastic products	4.35%	5.02%	29.65%	24.19%	8.03%	9.38%
Manufacture of glass and ceramic goods	10.47%	15.04%	19.81%	22.84%	6.49%	6.42%
Manufacture of cement, bricks, tiles, flags	0.47%	3.15%	7.09%	7.39%	2.31%	2.27%
Manufacture of concrete and cement products	0.13%	0.11%	11.97%	14.10%	1.99%	2.83%
Manufacture of basic ferrous metals	0.03%	0.05%	24.91%	30.93%	8.45%	9.70%
First processing of iron and steel	0.08%	0.19%	28.95%	34.05%	5.96%	4.77%
Manufacture of basic non-ferrous metals	1.81%	0.93%	27.54%	35.06%	12.81%	6.02%
Casting of metal products	1.93%	0.61%	17.14%	14.42%	5.42%	8.37%
Manufacture of construct. materials of metal	0.11%	0.11%	29.13%	20.01%	3.07%	4.31%
Manufacture of hand tools, metal packaging	3.32%	5.79%	26.06%	24.06%	5.87%	5.84%
Manufacture of marine engines, compressors	0.47%	0.77%	20.22%	22.19%	3.12%	4.38%
Manufacture of other general machinery	0.64%	1.64%	22.16%	24.40%	2.37%	3.50%
Manufacture of agricultural machinery	3.30%	3.09%	24.81%	26.94%	2.05%	2.53%
Manufacture of machinery for industries	2.31%	3.66%	21.97%	23.37%	3.11%	3.07%
Manufacture of domestic appliances	25.57%	35.37%	32.30%	30.37%	7.17%	5.86%
Manufacture of office machinery	14.11%	37.35%	21.07%	31.47%	4.43%	6.24%
Manufacture of other electrical machinery	3.08%	2.83%	22.89%	28.91%	5.73%	5.18%
Manufacture of communication equipment	25.22%	21.42%	25.97%	33.42%	4.83%	5.77%
Manufacture of medical and optical instruments	7.76%	6.44%	21.35%	21.23%	6.46%	6.91%
Manufacture of motor vehicles	91.82%	139.32%	30.43%	31.73%	2.67%	6.07%
Building and repairing of ships and boats	0.80%	1.28%	27.17%	28.39%	5.06%	4.74%
Manufacture of transport equipment excl. ships	24.71%	29.17%	33.06%	36.80%	2.18%	4.33%
Manufacture of furniture	7.22%	7.27%	20.60%	22.25%	2.55%	4.41%
Manufacture of toys, gold and silver articles	26.82%	37.11%	17.65%	23.93%	3.92%	4.58%
Total:	10.79%	15.78%	20.63%	22.56%	4.14%	4.80%

Notes: The average share of import in columns (1) and (2) is computed as the total value of import of final goods and services divided by the total value of production for each industry for the periods 1980-1992 and 1993-2004. Similarly, the average share of outsourcing in columns (3) and (4) is computed as the total value of imported inputs for production divided by the total value of production for each industry for the two periods. Finally, the average share of labour immigration in columns (5) and (6) is computed as the number of full-time employed immigrants divided by the total number of full-time workers for each industry for the two periods.

5. Estimation Strategy

In this section, I present the estimation procedure used for providing empirical evidence on the components from the decomposition of the slope of the Phillips curve, and for testing the effect of globalization on the Phillips curve. For these purposes, I estimate industry-specific Phillips curves that allow me to conduct detailed analyses at the industrial level. In the first stage of the empirical analysis, it is tested to what extent the decline in the sensitivity of wages to the unemployment gap is driven by changes in the slopes of industry-specific Phillips curves and changes in the employment shares between industries. In the second stage, it is tested how far globalization through a number of channels of economic openness influences the slope of the aggregate Phillips curve.

5.1. Sensitivity of wages to the unemployment gap

The first stage of the empirical analysis builds on an industry-specific Phillips curve specification, where the average wage change for a given industry is determined by the rate of productivity for that industry and the unemployment gap for the entire economy. By assuming that Δw_{it} is the percentage change of the real wage for industry i between the years $t-1$ and t, I use the following specification for the first stage of the analysis, which is the empirical version of (2) in the theoretical decomposition:

$$\Delta w_{it} = \alpha_{i\tau} - \beta_{i\tau}\left(u_t - u_t^*\right) + \varepsilon_{it} \qquad (5)$$

The first term on the right-hand side in (5) represents the effect of productivity increases on the change of real wages in the industry. We assume that the rate of productivity is allowed to vary between the two periods in the analyses (1980-1992 and 1993-2006), but is constant in each of the two periods. Thus, $\alpha_{i\tau}$ is the effect of productivity increases on the average annual rate of wage changes for industry i in sub-period τ, where $\tau = 1$ refers to the period 1980-1992 while $\tau = 2$ refers to the period 1993-2006.

The second term on the right-hand side represents the influence of the unemployment gap, $(u_t - u_t^*)$, where u_t is the actual rate of unemployment of the economy in year t, and u_t^* is the structural rate of unemployment of the economy in year t. $\beta_{i\tau}$ measures the sensitivity of wages to the unemployment gap, where a high value of $\beta_{i\tau}$ indicates that the unemployment gap has a large impact on the rate of wage changes. We assume that $\beta_{i\tau}$ is allowed to vary across industries as well as between the two periods.

The last term on the right-hand side is the 'white noise' part of the wage change for industry i between the years $t-1$ and t. ε_{it} includes other conditions than the productivity increases and unemployment gap that, for some reason, induce the wage change to become particularly high or low in industry i in a given year.

From the specification in (5), I am able to estimate α_{it} and β_{it} for 96 industries using data on the average rates of annual wage changes for each industry and the unemployment gap for the entire economy. Based on the estimated coefficients, I analyze whether the sensitivity of wages to the unemployment gap has been different across industries over the last two decades. Moreover, I use the estimated values of β_i, and the employment shares for each industry, to provide empirical evidence on the "within-industry effect" and "between-industry effect" from the decomposition of the slope of the aggregate Phillips curve.

5.2. Globalization and the slope of the Phillips curve

In the second stage of the empirical analysis, the estimated values of β_i are used to analyze the effect of globalization on the slope of the aggregate Phillips curve. Specifically, I set up the following two specifications for an industry to test how far globalization through the three channels of economic openness affects the change of the wage sensitivity to the unemployment gap:

$$\Delta \tilde{\beta}_i = \gamma_0 + \gamma_1 \Delta IM_i + \gamma_2 \Delta OUT_i + \gamma_3 \Delta FOR_i + \Delta \varepsilon_i \tag{6A}$$

$$\Delta \tilde{\beta}_i = \delta_0 + \delta_1 IM_{i,1980} + \delta_2 OUT_{i,1980} + \delta_3 FOR_{i,1980} + \Delta \varepsilon_{i,1980} \tag{6B}$$

In (6A), the first variable on the right-hand side is ΔIM_i, which represents the change of the average share of import of final goods and services in production for industry i between the periods 1980-1992 and 1993-2004. Similarly, ΔOUT_i is the change of the average share of import of intermediates in production (outsourcing) for industry i over the two periods. Finally, ΔFOR_i is the change of the average share of immigrants in total employment for industry i over the two periods. By relating the average changes of the estimated industry-specific Phillips curve slopes between the two periods to the average changes of the three measures of economic openness, I test the effect of globalization on the slope of the Phillips curve for the 54 industries in the manufacturing sector.

In (6B), I relate the estimated industry-specific Phillips curve slopes between the two periods 1980-1992 and 1993-2006 to the values of the three measures of economic openness in 1980 for the 54 industries in the manufacturing sector. This allows me to test whether the industries, which were most open in 1980, are also the industries that have later had the greatest access to foreign trade and labour, and thus have experienced the largest decline in the wage sensitivity to the unemployment gap. In both tests, I expect the estimates of the measures of economic openness to be negative if globalization tends to weaken the linkage between wage changes and the unemployment gap.

6. Empirical Results

This section presents the results of the estimations. Subsection 6.1 presents the empirical evidence on the decomposition of the slope of the Phillips curve, while Subsection 6.2 contains the estimation results from estimating the specifications related to the analyses on globalization effects.

6.1. Estimation and decomposition of the slope of the Phillips curve

Based on estimates from 96 industries, Table 3 below contains the results of the estimated wage sensitivity to the unemployment gap for seven groups of industries and for the economy as a whole. The third and fourth columns show the averages of the sensitivity of wages to the unemployment gap for the two periods 1980-1992 and 1993-2006, respectively. The estimates measure the percentage increase in the average wage for a given group of industries related to a decline in the unemployment gap of the economy of 1 percentage point. For instance, it is shown for the first period that a decline in the unemployment gap of 1 percentage point increases the average wage for industries in the manufacturing sector by 0.86%.

Table 3: Estimates of wage sensitivity to the unemployment gap

	(1) (2) Number of employees (Average)		(3) (4) Wage sensitivity to the unemployment gap (Average)	
Groups of industries:	1980-1992	1993-2006	1980-1992	1993-2006
Agriculture, etc.	33,308	32,148	0.80%	-0.17%
Manufacturing	399,118	384,130	0.86%	0.24%
Construction	121,004	130,456	1.35%	0.07%
Wholesale and retail sale	260,655	304,134	0.91%	-0.12%
Transport, post and telecom.	100,750	130,632	0.73%	0.06%
Financial intermediate and insurance	66,763	66,800	0.48%	0.49%
Other services	95,395	151,054	0.97%	0.14%
Total:	1,076,993	1,199,354	0.86%	0.16%

Notes: The seven groups of industries are constructed from 96 underlying industries included in the standard 130-classification in the Danish national accounts. The numbers of employees in columns (1) and (2) are computed as simple averages of the average numbers of full-time workers for underlying industries for the periods 1980-1992 and 1993-2006. The wage sensitivity to the unemployment gap measures the estimated increase in average wages in percent associated with a decline in the unemployment gap of the entire economy of 1 percent. The numbers in columns (3) and (4) are computed as weighted averages of the sensitivity of wages to the unemployment gap for underlying industries for the two periods.

It appears from Table 3 that there has been a decline in the sensitivity of wages to the unemployment gap for most industries in the Danish economy between the two periods. In the first period, there is a distinct inverse relationship between the wage changes and the unemployment gap for all industries in the economy, and particularly for the construction sector. However, in the second period, the wage increases in most industries have become far less sensitive to changes in the unemployment gap with the only exception being industries in the financial sector. Thus, there is a tendency for wage changes to no longer depend on changes in the activity level of the economy.

From the decomposition in Section 3, the aggregate Phillips curve is specified as a weighted average of all industry-specific Phillips curves in the economy. As a result, the change in the wage sensitivity to the unemployment gap of the economy is therefore driven by changes in the slopes of industry-specific Phillips curves and changes in the employment shares between industries, respectively. Table 4 reports the results from the decomposition of the decline of the slope of the Phillips curve observed over the two periods for the seven groups of industries and the economy as a whole:

Table 4: Decomposition of the slope of the Phillips curve

	(1)	(2)	(3)
	Shares of total change of the slope of the Phillips curve between 1980-1992 and 1993-2006		
Groups of industries:	Within effect	Between effect	Total effect
Agriculture, etc.	100.28%	-0.28%	100.00%
Manufacturing	98.11%	1.89%	100.00%
Construction	100.00%	0.00%	100.00%
Whole sale and retail sale	100.34%	-0.34%	100.00%
Transport, post and telecom.	98.34%	1.66%	100.00%
Financial intermediate and insurance	99.66%	0.34%	100.00%
Other services	99.94%	0.06%	100.00%
Total:	99.10%	0.90%	100.00%

Notes: The seven groups of industries are constructed from 96 underlying industries included in the standard 130-classification in the Danish national accounts. The average slopes of the (group) industry-specific Phillips curves are weighted by the industry size (average number of employees for each industry for the periods 1980-1992 and 1993-2006).

It is shown very clearly that most of the observed decline of the wage sensitivity to the unemployment gap can be ascribed to changes in the slopes of industry-specific Phillips curves, while changes in the employment shares between industries are of only very limited importance. Specifically, I find that more than 99% of the decline of the slope of the aggregate Phillips curve is caused by the "within-industry effect", while the "between-industry effect" is estimated to account for less than 1%. This is confirmed by the results from different groups of industries, which show that the 'within-industry effect' is on average 98-

100%.[6] Thus, there is a tendency for the wage sensitivity to the unemployment gap to decline in the same way among most groups of industries in Denmark.

6.2. Does globalization affect the slope of the Phillips curve?

Based on the estimates of wage sensitivity to the unemployment gap for the 54 industries in the manufacturing sector, Table 5 contains the results of estimating the specification on globalization effects in (5A), using weighted least squares by the industry size. I ran several regressions using different combinations of the three measures of economic openness:

Table 5: Changes in measures of economic openness and wage sensitivity to the unemployment gap, 1980-2004

	(1)	(2)	(3)	(4)	(5)	(6)	(7)	(8)
Dependent variable: Change of wage sensitivity to the unemployment gap								
Change in share of import	0.2923			0.0726	-0.1452		-0.3085	0.2284
	(0.37)			(0.09)	(-0.19)		(-0.41)	(0.47)
Change in share of outsourcing		3.8454		3.8120		3.0837	3.2066	2.5912
		(1.76)		(1.67)		(1.50)	(1.53)	(1.77)
Change in share of labour immigration			18.1076		18.3268	17.0040	17.4298	-2.827
			(3.10)**		(3.05)**	(2.92)††	(2.93)**	(-0.62)
R-squared	0.0026	0.0563	0.1562	0.0564	0.1568	0.1918	0.1945	0.0812
Observations	54	54	54	54	54	54	54	53

Notes: The estimations in columns (1)-(7) are based on the calculated wage sensitivity to the unemployment gap for the 54 industries in the manufacturing sector for the periods 1980-1992 and 1993-2004, where observations are weighted by the industry size. In column (8), the industry for "production of meat and meat products" is excluded from the analysis. The explanatory variables are: 1) Change in the import-production ratio; 2) Change in the outsourcing-production ratio, and 3) Change in the ratio between the number of full-time employed immigrants and the total number of full-time workers. "+" and "-" indicate whether the estimated effect of a variable on the change of the wage sensitivity to the unemployment gap is positive or negative. t-values in parentheses. ** and * indicate significance at the 1% and 5% level, respectively.

In columns (1)-(3), I ran the regressions separately for each of the three measures of economic openness to test whether higher import, outsourcing and labour immigration reduce the sensitivity of wages to the unemployment gap and thereby flatten the slope of the Phillips curve. Surprisingly, I find a positive

---

[6] Actually, I find the 'within-industry effect' to be higher than 100% for the industry groups: 'agriculture, etc.' (100.28%) and 'wholesale and retail sale' (100.34%).

relationship between the change of the sensitivity of wages and the change of each of the three measures of economic openness over the periods 1980-1992 and 1993-2004, although it is only the effect of labour immigration that is significant.[7] The significant positive effect of labour immigration on the slope of the Phillips curve is confirmed by the results in columns (4)-(7), where I ran the regressions for a number of combinations of the three measures of economic openness. However, it is important to mention that the industry of "production of meat and meat products" is crucial for the estimated effects. Specifically, if this industry is excluded from the regressions, it appears from column (8) that labour immigration no longer has a significantly positive effect on the slope of the Phillips curve.

Apart from other industries, the industry of "production of meat and meat products" has experienced a simultaneous increase in the sensitivity of wages to the unemployment gap and labour immigration over the two periods.[8] Such a positive relationship for some industries could be explained by the fact that firms have an extra incentive to increase their employment of foreign labour during upswings with large wage increases. This gives rise to the existence of a statistical positive relationship between the change of the wage sensitivity to the unemployment gap and the change of labour immigration – even in situations where a higher utilization of foreign labour tends to offset wage increases for a given unemployment gap. As a result, it is not possible to test the effect of labour immigration on the slope of the Phillips curve by comparing the change of wage sensitivity to the unemployment gap with the change of utilization of foreign labour.

Another way to test whether an easier access to international trade and foreign labour affects the wage sensitivity to the unemployment gap, is thus to use measures of economic openness that are not affected by the formation of wages in the estimation period. To do this, I relate the change of the estimates of wage sensitivity to the unemployment gap for the two periods 1980-1992 and 1993-2006 to the values of the three measures of economic openness for the first year of the data period, 1980, for the 54 industries in the manufacturing sector. In Table 6 below, I present the results of estimating the specification in (6B), using weighted least squares by the industry size. Again, I ran several regressions:

---

[7] Similarly, I find a significantly positive effect of labour immigration on the slope of the Phillips curve using data for the periods 1980-1992 and 1993-2006.

[8] More specifically, over the periods 1980-1992 and 1993-2004, the sensitivity of wages to the unemployment gap has increased from 0.93% to 2.36%, while the share of foreign labour in relation to the total employment has increased from 2.72% to 7.00%.

Table 6: International trade, foreign labour and wage sensitivity to the unemployment gap, 1980-2006

	(1)	(2)	(3)	(4)	(5)	(6)	(7)	(8)
Dependent variable: Change of wage sensitivity to the unemployment gap								
Share of import	-0.1938 (-0.24)			0.3758 (0.50)	-0.1772 (-0.22)		0.4168 (0.56)	0.6214 (1.21)
Share of outsourcing		-2.9593 (-3.45)**		-3.0582 (-3.45)**		-3.4699 (-3.66)**	-3.5800 (-3.67)**	-1.0585 (-1.40)
Share of labour immigration			-1.3501 (-0.37)		-1.3032 (-0.35)	4.4745 (1.23)	4.5658 (1.24)	3.9274 (1.55)
R-squared	0.0011	0.1864	0.0026	0.1904	0.0036	0.2098	0.2148	0.0782
Observations	54	54	54	54	54	54	54	53

Notes: The estimations in columns (1)-(7) are based on the calculated wage sensitivity to the unemployment gap for the 54 industries in the manufacturing sector for the periods 1980-1992 and 1993-2006, where observations are weighted by the industry size. In column (8), the industry for "production of meat and meat products" is excluded from the analysis. The explanatory variables are: 1) Import-production ratio in 1980; 2) Outsourcing-production ratio in 1980, and 3) The ratio between the number of full-time employed immigrants and the total number of full-time workers in 1980. "+" and "-" indicate whether the estimated effect of a variable on the change of the wage sensitivity to the unemployment gap is positive or negative. t values in parentheses. ** and * indicate significance at the 1% and 5% level, respectively.
Source: Statistics Denmark.

In columns (1)-(3), I ran the regressions including each of the three measures of economic openness to test whether the industries which were most open in 1980 have experienced the largest decline of the wage sensitivity to the unemployment gap over the two periods. While there is no significant relationship between the measures of import and labour immigration in 1980 and the following change of the wage sensitivity to the unemployment gap, I do find a significantly negative effect of outsourcing in 1980 on the sensitivity of wages to the unemployment gap. This significantly negative effect of outsourcing on the slope of the Phillips curve is confirmed by the results in columns (4)-(7) where I ran the regressions including different combinations of the 1980-levels of import, outsourcing and labour immigration. However, it is important to mention that the results are not particularly robust, and that the industry of "production of meat and meat products" is again crucial for the estimated effects. If this industry is excluded from the regression, it appears from column (8) that the negative effect of outsourcing on the slope of the Phillips curve is no longer significant.

7. Conclusion

Since the beginning of the 1990s, the sensitivity of wages to the unemployment gap has declined considerably in most industries in Denmark. Especially for industries in the construction, manufacturing, and wholesale and retail sale sectors, the tendency for lower wage increases at high rates of unemployment has been striking, whereas the wage formation has been almost unchanged for industries in the financial sector in the same period.

In the first part of the paper, industry-specific Phillips curves were estimated to test whether the recent years' finding of the weaker link between aggregate wage changes and the unemployment gap in Denmark is due to changes within industries or should instead be ascribed to changes in the relative sizes of industries. It was shown that the decline in the wage sensitivity to the unemployment gap is caused almost entirely by changes in the slopes of industry-specific Phillips curves ("within-industry-effect"), whereas changes in the employment shares between industries ("between-industry effect") are of only very limited importance.

In the second part of the paper, the estimates of the slopes of industry-specific Phillips curves were related to three measures of economic openness to test how far globalization through a variety of channels influences the slope of the Phillips curve for Denmark. It was found that industries in the manufacturing sector with an easier access to international outsourcing show weaker wage responses to the unemployment gap, whereas access to import of foreign final goods and foreign labour seem to have no effect on the slope of the Phillips curve. However, it is important to mention these results are not very clear or robust and that, hence, there are a number of caveats to my conclusions.

References

Abowd, J.M. and F. Kramarz (1999): "The Analysis of Labor Markets using Matched Employer-Employee Data", in Ashenfelter and Cards (eds.), *Handbook of Labor Economics*, Vol. 3B, Amsterdam: Elsevier Science, 2629-2710.

Ball, L. (2006): "Has Globalization Changed Inflation?", NBER working paper, No. 12687.

Bean, C. (2006): "Globalization and Inflation", *Bank of England Quarterly Bulletin*, Q4, 468-475.

Bentolila, S., J. Dolado and J.F. Kimeno (2007): "Does Immigration Affect the Phillips Curve? Some Evidence from Spain", CEPR discussion paper, No. 6604.

Borio, C. and A. Filardo (2007): "Globalization and Inflation: New Cross-Country Evidence on the Global Determinants of Domestic Inflation", BIS, No. 227.

Bowdler, C. (2003): "Openness and the Output-Inflation Tradeoff", Money Macro and Finance Research Group Conference 2003, No. 7.

Danish Economic Council (2008): "Danish Economy, Autumn 2008", Copenhagen.

Dexter, A.S., M.D. Levi and B.R. Nault (2005): "International Trade and the Connection Between Excess Demand and Inflation", *Review of International Economics*, Vol. 13, No. 4, 699-708.

Gamber, E.N. and J.H. Hung (2001): "Has the Rise in Globalization Reduced U.S. Inflation in the 1990s?", *Economic Inquiry*, Vol. 39, No. 1, 58-73.

Helbling, T., F. Jaumotte and M. Sommer (2006): "How Has Globalization Affected Inflation?", IMF World Economic Outlook, Chapter III, April.

Ihrig, J., S.B. Kamin, D. Lindner and J. Marquez (2007): "Some Simple Tests of the Globalization and Inflation Hypothesis", Board of Governors International Finance Discussion Paper, No. 893.

Mishkin, R. (2007): "Inflation Dynamics", NBER working paper, No. 13147.

Munch, J.R. and J.R. Skaksen (2008): "Specialization, Outsourcing and Wages", *Review of International Economics*. Forthcoming.

Pain, N., I. Koske and M. Sollie (2006): "Globalization and inflation in the OECD economies", OECD Economics Department, working paper, No. 524.

Phillips, A.W. (1958): "The Relationship between Unemployment and the Rate of Change of Money Wages in the United Kingdom 1861-1957", *Economica*, Vol. 25, 283-299.

Razin, A and C. Yuen (2002): "The New Keynesian Phillips curve: Closed Economy versus Open Economy", *Economic Letters*, Vol. 75 (2002), 1-9.

Razin, A. and A. Binyamini (2007): "Flattening Inflation-Output Tradeoff and Enhanced Anti-Inflation Policy as an Equilibrium Outcome of Globalization", HKIMR working paper, No. 23/2007.

Rodrik, D. (1997): "Has Globalization Gone Too Far?" Washington DC: Institute for International Economics.

Rogoff, K. (2006): "The impact of globalization on monetary policy", presented at the Federal Reserve Bank of Kansas City 30th Annual Economic Symposium, Jackson Hole, Wyoming.

Temple, J. (2002): "Openness, inflation and the Phillips curve: a puzzle", *Journal of Money, Credit and Banking*, Vol. 34, No. 2, 450-468.

Publications in English from the Rockwool Foundation Research Unit

Time and Consumption
Edited by Gunnar Viby Mogensen. With contributions by Søren Brodersen, Thomas Gelting, Niels Buus Kristensen, Eszter Körmendi, Lisbeth Pedersen, Benedicte Madsen. Niels Ploug, Erik Ib Schmidt, Rewal Schmidt Sørensen, and Gunnar Viby Mogensen (Statistics Denmark, Copenhagen. 1990)

Danes and Their Politicians
By Gunnar Viby Mogensen (Aarhus University Press. 1993)

Solidarity or Egoism?
By Douglas A. Hibbs (Aarhus University Press. 1993)

Welfare and Work Incentives. A North European Perspective
Edited by A.B. Atkinson and Gunnar Viby Mogensen. With Contributions by A.B. Atkinson, Richard Blundell, Björn Gustafsson, Anders Klevmarken, Peder J. Pedersen, and Klaus Zimmermann (Oxford University Press. 1993)

Unemployment and Flexibility on the Danish Labour Market
By Gunnar Viby Mogensen (Statistics Denmark, Copenhagen. 1994)

On the Measurement of a Welfare Indicator for Denmark 1970-1990
By Peter Rørmose Jensen and Elisabeth Møllgaard (Statistics Denmark, Copenhagen. 1995)

The Shadow Economy in Denmark 1994. Measurement and Results
By Gunnar Viby Mogensen, Hans Kurt Kvist, Eszter Körmendi, and Søren Pedersen (Statistics Denmark, Copenhagen. 1995)

Work Incentives in the Danish Welfare State: New Empirical Evidence
Edited by Gunnar Viby Mogensen. With contributions by Søren Brodersen, Lisbeth Pedersen, Peder J. Pedersen, Søren Pedersen, and Nina Smith (Aarhus University Press. 1995)

Actual and Potential Recipients of Welfare Benefits with a Focus on Housing Benefits, 1987-1992
By Hans Hansen and Marie Louise Hultin (Statistics Denmark, Copenhagen. 1997)

The Shadow Economy in Western Europe. Measurement and Results for Selected Countries
By Søren Pedersen. With contributions by Esben Dalgaard and Gunnar Viby Mogensen (Statistics Denmark, Copenhagen. 1998)

Immigration to Denmark. International and National Perspectives
By David Coleman and Eskil Wadensjö. With contributions by Bent Jensen and Søren Pedersen (Aarhus University Press. 1999)

Nature as a Political Issue in the Classical Industrial Society: The Environmental Debate in the Danish Press from the 1870s to the 1970s
By Bent Jensen (Statistics Denmark, Copenhagen. 2000)

Foreigners in the Danish newspaper debate from the 1870s to the 1990s
By Bent Jensen (Statistics Denmark, Copenhagen. 2001)

The integration of non-Western immigrants in a Scandinavian labour market: The Danish experience
By Marie Louise Schultz-Nielsen. With contributions by Olaf Ingerslev, Claus Larsen, Gunnar Viby Mogensen, Niels-Kenneth Nielsen, Søren Pedersen, and Eskil Wadensjö (Statistics Denmark, Copenhagen. 2001)

Immigration and the public sector in Denmark
By Eskil Wadensjö and Helena Orrje (Aarhus University Press. 2002)

Social security in Denmark and Germany – with a focus on access conditions for refugees and immigrants. A comparative study
By Hans Hansen, Helle Cwarzko Jensen, Claus Larsen, and Niels-Kenneth Nielsen (Statistics Denmark, Copenhagen. 2002)

The Shadow Economy in Germany, Great Britain, and Scandinavia. A Measurement Based on Questionnaire Surveys
By Søren Pedersen (Statistics Denmark, Copenhagen. 2003)

Do-it-yourself work in North-Western Europe. Maintenance and improvement of homes
By Søren Brodersen (Statistics Denmark, Copenhagen. 2003)

Migrants, Work, and the Welfare State
Edited by Torben Tranæs and Klaus F. Zimmermann. With contributions by Thomas Bauer, Amelie Constant, Horst Entorf, Christer Gerdes, Claus Larsen, Poul Chr. Matthiessen, Niels-Kenneth Nielsen, Marie Louise Schultz-Nielsen, and Eskil Wadensjö (University Press of Southern Denmark. 2004)

Black Activities in Germany in 2001 and in 2004. A Comparison Based on Survey Data
By Lars P. Feld and Claus Larsen (Statistics Denmark, Copenhagen. 2005)

From Asylum Seeker to Refugee to Family Reunification. Welfare Payments in These Situations in Various Western Countries
By Hans Hansen (Statistics Denmark, Copenhagen. 2006)

A Comparison of Welfare Payments to Asylum Seekers, Refugees, and Reunified Families. In Selected European Countries and in Canada
By Torben Tranæs, Bent Jensen, and Mark Gervasini Nielsen (Statistics Denmark, Copenhagen. 2006)

Employment Effects of Reducing Welfare to Refugees
By Duy T. Huynh, Marie Louise Schultz-Nielsen, and Torben Tranæs (The Rockwool Foundation Research Unit. 2007)

Determination of Net Transfers for Immigrants in Germany
By Christer Gerdes (The Rockwool Foundation Research Unit. 2007)

What happens to the Employment of Native Co-Workers when Immigrants are Hired?
By Nikolaj Malchow-Møller, Jakob Roland Munch, and Jan Rose Skaksen (The Rockwool Foundation Research Unit. 2007)

Immigrants at the Workplace and the Wages of Native Workers
By Nikolaj Malchow-Møller, Jakob Roland Munch, and Jan Rose Skaksen (The Rockwool Foundation Research Unit. 2007)

Crime and Partnerships
By Michael Svarer (University Press of Southern Denmark, The Rockwool Foundation Research Unit. 2008)

Immigrant and Native Children's Cognitive Outcomes and the Effect of Ethnic Concentration in Danish Schools
By Peter Jensen and Astrid Würtz Rasmussen (University Press of Southern Denmark, The Rockwool Foundation Research Unit. 2008)

The Unemployed in the Danish Newspaper Debate from the 1840s to the 1990s
By Bent Jensen (University Press of Southern Denmark, The Rockwool Foundation Research Unit. 2008)

Source Country Differences in Test Score Gaps: Evidence from Denmark
By Beatrice Schindler Rangvid (University Press of Southern Denmark, The Rockwool Foundation Research Unit. 2008)

Has Globalization Changed the Phillips Curve? Industry-Level Evidence on the Effect of the Unemployment Gap on Wages
By Claus Aastrup Jensen (University Press of Southern Denmark, The Rockwool Foundation Research Unit. 2009)

Emigration of Immigrants – A Duration Analysis
By Sanne Schroll (University Press of Southern Denmark, The Rockwool Foundation Research Unit. 2009)

The Rockwool Foundation Research Unit on the Internet

Completely updated information, e.g. about the latest projects of the Research Unit, can be found on the Internet on the home page of the Research Unit at the address:

www.rff.dk

The home page includes in a Danish and an English version:

- a commented survey of publications stating distributors of the books of the Research Unit

- survey of research projects

- information about the organization and staff of the Research Unit

- information about data base and choice of method and

- newsletters from the Research Unit

Printed newsletters from the Rockwool Foundation Research Unit can also be ordered free of charge on telephone +45 39 17 38 32.